CREATING PROSPERITY & FINANCIAL PEACE

GRAHAM HOWARTH
FINANCIAL COACH

Zeta Publishing, Inc
P.O. Box 953
Silver Springs, FL 34489
www.zetapublishing.com

The views expressed in this work are solely those of the author and do not necessarily reflect the views of the publisher, and the publisher hereby disclaims any responsibility for them.

Ordering Information:
Quantity sales. Special discounts are available on quantity purchases by corporations, associations, and others. For details, contact the publisher at the address above.
Orders by U.S. trade bookstores and wholesalers. Please contact Zeta Publishing: Tel: (352) 694-2553; Fax: (352) 694-1791 or visit www.zetapublishing.com

First published by iUniverse

Rev. Date: Oct, 2019

ISBN: 978-1-950340-18-7 (sc)
ISBN: 978-1-950340-19-4 (e)

Library of Congress: 2019915753
Printed in the United States of America

Zeta Publishing

Dedication

W. Clement Stone said "What the mind of a man can conceive and believe... It can achieve."

The very fact that you are holding this book in your hands is evidence that no truer words were ever spoken. I believe my reason for being here on Earth, is to have a positive purpose, to help people create dreams and achieve prosperity.

At times the dreams I had and the goals I set seemed hopeless. For the life of me I could not see the means to their manifestation. But the love of my family, Shelley, Allie and Katie and God's beautiful words, "ask and ye shall receive," have spurred me on and kept me believing in myself.

Many thanks to David and Jacqueline Findlay, who have helped not only with the creation of this book, but have been there to help guide my family and I in many different situations over the years.

For all those who doubted this project would come to a conclusion, Thank You. The doubts I heard in your voices inspired me to push harder and think deeper in an effort to accomplish this goal. It has taken me over a decade to achieve this goal. I have learned if you can visualize your dreams, put pen to paper and hold that dream in your hand, anything is possible.

I have found the more people you tell about a project, the more pressure you exert upon your self to see the project through to the end.

Introduction

"Success seems to be largely a matter of hanging on after others have let go."

-*William Feather*

Everything one does in life starts with single thought. This gift that people have to process thoughts is what differentiates humans from other species of animals. Simple thoughts such as, should I get out of bed, should I have a coffee, that apple looks good, even just raising an arm, everything originates from a single thought. It is one of the most valuable tools people have.

With each thought human beings have a choice. Blaming others for our lack of achievement or our poor choice is nothing more than an excuse. Ask yourself, "Does my behavior match my intentions?" Watch yourself in action, take a long hard look at yourself, what do you see?

At that point, you need to take responsibility for the way your life is. What are the choices you have made that brought you to this point? If you could live life over, what changes would you make? Look at your life experiences. That will give you an awareness of your decision-making prowess, also known as your thought processes.

It takes great inner strength to take a serious look at

ourselves and the way we are living our lives and then to make timely corrections. As we look at our failures as human beings, we see a need to change, and as human beings it is in our nature to resist change. I am a believer that you cannot actually change who you are, but you can grow from where you are now and transform yourself to the person you want to be.

Let's try our first exercise here;

Exercise 1.
On a piece of paper write your obituary. Write what you want people to say about you when you are gone. Put this obituary in an envelope, seal and address it to yourself. Once you have completed all the exercises in this book open the envelope and compare yourself to what you have written in the obituary. Are you doing the things necessary in your life to fulfill what your obituary says?

This is what the journey of life is about: acknowledging our weaknesses and the choices we have made, learning and growing from them, and eventually achieving prosperity.

I have been told by many successful business owners and presidents of major corporations that if at some point you don't fail, you will never be successful," and trust me, I have had my share of failures. However, I learned a valuable lesson from each failure. Failing at something does not make you a failure. By failing you are actually growing as a person and you can use the knowledge you gain from the experience elsewhere in your life. Eventually you will succeed. Failing is a lesson of life. It is another event that will help shape your destiny.

Back in the 1980's I started an import/export company.

I bought a course of an infomercial on television and I thought I was going to be a millionaire. Through the direction of this course I was able to contact certain individuals that were looking for representation for their products here in Canada. I was able to find a product, sign an exclusive rights contract for all of Canada, I thought I was set.

With the help of a friend, I got my first customer in Toronto covering six stores. I found if I wanted to grow my business I must purchase larger quanitities myself in order to receive a price break, thus, allowing me to give more competitive price to my customers.

So I purchased $7,000 of merchandise. Just after I received the product from the company I started receiving complaints about the quality and how the product was falling apart. It wasn't long after that the people who invented and manufactured the product went out of business.

Here I was, an assistant manager at a retail store not making a lot of money, but losing a lot.

Not having experience at importing / exporting or wholesaling merchandise cost me a lot of time, money and credibility. My first failure, or was it? I decided at that point, should I be able to find another product I would do things differently. I started learning by interviewing people or friends of people I know how purchasing in the retail industry works. If I didn't know a person I would ask people if they knew somebody who could help me. Later in my career I recognized this as a valuable lesson in the art of networking.

I decided to use other people's money instead of my own. If I got an order I would ask the bank to lend me money for thirty to sixty days based on the strength of a purchase order. Most banks are open to this providing you have a solid business plan and your client is well established.

I also decided, instead of just signing a contract to secure a product, the contract had to be just as beneficial to me as the other party. If a person or company thinks they can get the better of you in a signed document, they almost always will. So I educated myself on negotiating techniques and business law so as to protect myself and not get taken advantage of again.

I took a bad experience, learned from my mistakes and moved forward. To date I still have products that I imported or developed in many major retailers across the United States and Canada.

If I had given up and listened to certain people who I thought were my friends, I would not have been able to write this book and share my experiences with you.

It is important for you to think in a positive, successful frame of mind. From this point forward act in a manner that makes you proud of yourself. If you think you're successful, you will be. If you think you're a failure, you will be a failure. Just a simple thing like changing your perception of the word "failing" to "growing" will help you overcome many of the barriers you have sub-consciously created over time. I believe the true character of a person lies not in failing, but in rising up again and going forward in life.

Think back to your childhood, you were probably kept in the comfort zone of your parents, your grandparents, your teachers and your community. How, might you ask? Think! How often, in their well-intentioned desire to protect you from harm, did they actually prevent you from expressing your true self and from taking the risks that are so essential to development?

Have you ever heard people say;

"Don't sing so loud you have a terrible voice"

" No"

"We have rules"

"You can't have that"

"If you do that, you will look silly"

"Why would you want to try that, if it doesn't work, you will look like a failure"

Just to name a few. They did not want you to experience "failure." Over time, their fears start to become your fears and you start to create barriers such as procrastination that keep you inside your comfort zone. Consequently, you begin to see life through a filter such as on a camera only letting through information related to your comfort zone.

Imagine when you were learning to walk, how often did your parents, grandparents or whomever stand over you hold your hands? How many times did you fail? Through trial and error you eventually learned to walk. In these circumstances we were encouraged and applauded for our efforts.

As you got older, when you were a child learning to ride a bike, how many times did you fall off, then get back on and try again? You failed, you learned, you failed, you learned and you finally succeeded.

Imagine if your parents or guardians allowed you to give up after falling the first time, what would you have missed out on in life?

it is this attitude of perseverance and positive re-enforcement that gave you the desire to want to improve and change things in your life. Why does this not continue through-out a childhood?

Are you doing the same for your children or are you stopping them from trying things because you're uncomfortable? Are you sending them mixed messages? It could be playing a sport that's to rough, opening a lemonade stand because it might be embarrassing to you, swimming or even reading certain types of books.

The problem rests with not knowing what mixed messages we as children picked from our parents or guardians that now sub- consciously affect our own behavior as adults.

Parents are telling their children to be Doctors or Lawyers instead of Actors or Writer's because they fear being looked at as failures themselves, should their children not succeed.

As you proceed through the steps that are laid out in this book you will learn who you are as a person, what it is in life you truly want and how to overcome the barriers that prevent you from getting what it is you desire.

The problem rests with not knowing what mixed messages we as children picked from our parents or guardians that now sub- consciously affect our own behavior as adults.

A question you will ask yourself (barrier) is, how do I find time and money for my dreams and goals and retire in peace? In later exercises I will show you how to find the extra money and time you already have and plan for your future.

My years of experience coaching people and financial planning have helped me develop exercises that will lead you through the process that of creating prosperity and financial peace. These exercises will help you move from chapter to chapter.

Please do not skip an exercise and think that you will go back and do it later. It won't work. I have provided space in the book for you to answer the questions. However, using a notebook will make it easier for you to give more detailed answers.

Take small steps, complete one exercise every few days, this will give you time to digest the information you have received.

By completing each exercise you are developing pieces of a plan on how to achieve prosperity and financial peace that will all come together at the end.

At this point, if you don't want to give 100% and be true to these exercises, put this book on the shelf with the other self-help books you have purchased and walk way, because it won't work for you. However, I promise you that you will transform yourself as a result of the inner work you do. How do I know? Because I transformed myself! Don't let that inner critic, that little you on your shoulder that might be about to awaken in your mind take over. This little you always start's to chatter when you have an opportunity to grow. It is nothing more than the voice of fear.

As you proceed through this book, I hope you will put to use the tools I have laid out to help you find the life that you want to lead and attain the peace that you truly want.

"I have not failed. I've just found 10,000 ways that won't work."

– Thomas Edison

CHAPTER 1
Knowing your sense of purpose.

"A journey of 1000 miles must start with a single step."
 -Lao Tzu *Chinese philosopher (604 BC - 531 BC)*

To be successful you must be motivated. Have a purpose, have a plan and have a sense of urgency.

We are motivated by our needs, but to meet these needs, we must evaluate and prioritize goals or tasks that will help us achieve success in meeting such needs. As you achieve a goal or task your priorities in achieving other goals or task may change.

The real reason most people don't feel successful is because they are not clear on who they are or what they want.

Awareness or knowing who you are and what you want is power, and with that power you can gain greater control over your life, your destiny.

When you seek success or happiness, in other words a life's purpose, this seeking should last a lifetime. Each time you reach a goal, your view of your life's purpose will possibly change.

Before you start to list your goals or what is important to you, you must first know who you are. By knowing who you are and what motivates you, you will create a more focused list that won't changed as much.

This second exercise is intended to give you a perspective of who you are as a person.

When a golfer is getting ready to putt the ball, he/she will look from afar on both sides of the hole to understand just how the ball will proceed to the hole once struck. When the golfer stands over the ball ready to make the putt the path or break looks completely different. You have to trust what you seen from afar is the correct path or break.

This exercise will help you begin to define who you are as a person. Once you have completed the exercise, read it aloud to yourself three times. When you read it aloud you will actually hear and start to believe who you are.

Just as the golfer looks at the path of the ball to the hole from two different sides, reading aloud will give you a different perspective than just reading it quietly to yourself.

Exercise 2
Answer the following questions.

List at least 7 answers for each question.

1. I am

_____
_____
_____
_____
_____

2. My beliefs are?

Morally I

_____
_____
_____
_____
_____

Spiritually I

_____
_____
_____
_____
_____

My values are

_____
_____
_____
_____
_____

3. I am motivated by

_____
_____
_____
_____
_____

4. I am here because

_____
_____
_____

_____

_____

5. I have been successful when

_____

_____

_____

_____

_____

6. Where have I failed

_____

_____

_____

_____

_____

Now write a statement of your beliefs combining all your answers, this will help you further process the information of you are. Once you have finished read it aloud three times.

Some examples to get you started are;

♦ morally, I am against abortion except in the case rape, I am for the death penalty.
♦ politically, taxes are too high. I believe in gun control. I trust in my politician.
♦ spiritually, I believe in God. I do not believe in organized religion.
♦ I value honesty, loyalty, money and friendship.
♦ I am motivated by fear and greed.

It is not society, the environment or the events in your life that determine who you are; it is your belief system that will determine your destiny. As your belief system directs the events that happen to you.

Chapter 2
What Would Make You Feel Prosperous

"Choose a job you love, and you will never have to work a day in your life."

-Confucius

It is usually easy to spot someone who has a life full of prosperity. They are generally authentic, fun, nice, ethical people with great relationships and values.

Having lots of money or possessions does not necessarily mean you have a prosperous life. Prosperity is not something that is given to us. It is a habit we create over time. The famous words "If I only had." Even the perfect situation might not be prosperous, as prosperity is the feeling of being satisfied and fulfilled in all areas of your life. Prosperity is different for everybody. Mother Theresa had a life full of prosperity, yet she had little money, she was always available when people needed her help. Her life's purpose was to help others.

If you are not currently feeling prosperous, even though you make a good income, you are probably going to have to change the quality of energy that surrounds your life and how you feel about yourself in order to find the comfort and joy that you seek. You are probably at a crossroads in life right now. Know that this is a wonderful time. Living in the unknown is when human beings are most alive, for this is a place where anything and everything is possible. If you open yourself to the world, the world will open up to you.

Exercise 3
What does prosperity mean to You?

_____

_____

_____

_____

_____

For you to have a life full of abundance and prosperity, you are going to have to learn how to access what you need in terms of people, things or money in order to feel satisfied. If you feel unworthy or deprived, it will be difficult for you to feel successful unless you learn two things.

1. What it is you truly want.
2. How to get it.

We as a species are happiest when we are growing, it's in our nature. When you fail, you grow. You have to fail to succeed.

All of us say we want more money or more possessions. But, when you sit down and think about your future, what is it you see? Is it being with a loved one, playing with your children, being happy at work, having lots of friends, owning a business, volunteering, all of these or something else?

Usually in someone's true dream, monetary possessions are secondary. You might see yourself playing in your yard with your spouse or children with a big house in the background, but the very fact that you first see your family as happy and healthy playing in the yard, well, I believe, that is your primary goal. The big house or fancy car in the background comes after your family.

If you are married or have a life partner, what are the goals of your spouse/partner or children? Are they in tune with your goals? Are you and your spouse/partner heading in the same direction or are you preventing each other from achieving what is important to each as an individual or a couple?

Exercise 4
Ask your spouse/partner or child to list some of their goals in life without any input from you at this time.

_____

_____

_____

_____

_____

_____

_____

_____

_____

Oh no, my goals are different than my spouse or partners. This is a perfect opportunity for you both to grow as a couple, discuss your difference. How can you make your partnership work? The use of a relationship coach could be of help to both of you here. Not a therapist, but a coach.

A coach will guide you to your own conclusions and not psychoanalyze the situation.

To achieve prosperity, you need to see prosperity as a creative process. That means you will have to travel inside yourself to find out who you are and define your values.

The key to living a prosperous life is the giving of yourself with no expectations of anything in return. In order to receive you must give, when you give you will receive in abundance.

When you wake-up every morning with a smile on your face and full of life, you have achieved prosperity.

CHAPTER 3
What is Financial Peace, Face Your Money Fears

"If you don't fear money and can accept volatility as part of your life, you will eventually become successful".
                                              -Graham Howarth

When I was growing up I remember hearing my parents discussing money. It usually wasn't very pleasant as money attitudes are both emotional and financial. These attitudes have a large impact on how we deal with money today. We either embrace or we reject these attitudes, but either way, we are the product of our parent's money. Most people are either savers or spenders. Savers save all their money usually paying cash for major purchases such as appliances or cars and sometimes miss out on what life has to offer. Spenders generally live paycheck to paycheck, enjoy life to a certain extent, but in private are always stressed about money. The goal is to find a balance between the two. Once you understand how either of your parent's money attitudes impact your life today you can begin to separate your own attitude from your parents.

Financial peace is different for everybody; it could be having enough money just to meet your obligations, or having an abundance of money to fill your life full of material possessions. It could be just a knowing you have enough money to live on when you retire, or being able to give to other family members or charities. Once you have truly recognized what it is you want out of life, whether it is material possessions, the emotional feeling of giving to others or that you simply have enough money to retire on. You are on your way to achieving financial peace.

We've all heard the terms "freedom 55," and "retire early." At the end of the day when people are on their deathbeds, the three most common things people regret are:

1. I should have looked back on my life more often.
2. I didn't take enough risks during my life.
3. I didn't give or show enough love.

This tells us most people don't learn how to live until they are close to dying.

In order to grow, we need to take time to look back and learn from the decisions we have made, what worked, what didn't.

I would rather try and fail than not to try it all. Don't leave deeds undone or words left unspoken as this will only lead to regret when it's too late to do anything about it.

The time has come to clear out our old subconscious.

Exercise 5

For this exercise you will your notepad and about 20 minutes.

Write down every money fear you have. Write down all that nasty stuff that keeps you awake at night.

The following are some examples to get you started.

1. If my spouse or partner dies, who will take care of me?
2. I am afraid I can't support my loved ones.
3. Where is my money invested?
4. I am afraid I won't have enough money when I retire.
5. Is my money invested in the right places?
6. I am afraid I won't be able to pay for my child's education.
7. I am afraid my parents might need long-term care.

_____
_____
_____
_____
_____
_____
_____

Well, join the club, we all have those fears. The problem is many people hang on to their fears long after the danger has passed. History shows us many of these fears will never actually materialize.

Put the questions to your Financial Advisor. If you don't have a Financial Advisor, get one. They are usually free.

Later in the book I will give guidance on finding a Financial Advisor.

CHAPTER 4

What is Prosperity and Financial Peace to You

"The difference between ordinary and extraordinary is that little extra."

-Jimmy Johnson

Since you have completed the previous exercises, you have a greater sense of who you are. In order to know what prosperity or financial peace means to you, you now have to look deeper inside yourself. It is easy to say I want lots of money, a big house or different career, but is it truly what you want? Find the passion within you for something big you would like to achieve and go for it!

This next exercise will help you determine what is important to you, your greatest regrets and what you would do if you could not fail. For this rapid fire exercise, it will work better for you by recording the questions on your phone or computer asking each question 8 times. You could also ask a close friend whom you can trust to ask you the questions below. Another option is to stand in front of a mirror and ask yourself the questions. Listen to the questions and answer as fast as you can without thinking or simply follow the steps that are laid out below, remember to be true to yourself or it will not work. Speak out loud and don't think about your answers. Answer the first thought that comes into your mind. You will think more clearly if you are standing while doing this exercise.

Your friend could also benefit from these questions.

Exercise 6

1. Find a quiet place to listen to the phone/computer or stand near a table with a pen and note book or tape recorder. Also have some form of clock that will beep after one minute.
2. Close your eyes, take a deep breath in through your nose and release slowly through your mouth, do this three times.
3. Open your eyes and look in the mirror.
4. Ask yourself out loud, **"The most important thing in my life is**_____" Answer yourself out loud immediately do not think.
5. Ask yourself the question again and answer...Do this for one minute. Do not write your answers.
6. At the end of one minute, write down the answers you remember, if you did not tape them.

_____

_____

_____

_____

_____

7. Reset your clock.
8. Repeat, the same procedures, but ask yourself this out loud. **"If I could live life over I would** _____" Answer out loud.
At the end of one minute, write down the answers

you remember.

_____

_____

_____

_____

_____

9. Reset the clock.
10. Using the same process as before, ask the following,
    "In my life, my biggest regret is _____**"**
    Answer out loud.
11. At the end of one minute, write down the answers
    you remember.

_____

_____

_____

_____

_____

12. Reset the clock.
13. Using the same process as before, ask the following,
    "If I knew I would not fail I would _____**?"**
    Answer out loud.
14. At the end of one minute, write down the answers
    you remember.

_____

_____

_____

_____

_____

Now that you have completed this exercise you should
have a defined list of values, goals, regrets and what is
important in your life. You are on the road to knowing

your true self.

Have you heard of the Six Degrees of separation? Simply put, you are potentially six people away from meeting someone you really want to meet, such as a movie star, the president of the United States etc. There is a game called "The Six Degrees of Kevin Bacon." In this game everybody in Hollywood can touch Kevin within six people, whether it is Studios, Directors, Producers or Actors. If you need the help of a certain individual and don't know that person directly, develop a list of people you know that might know people to get you that introduction.

Exercise 7

Take a look at each of your goals. Let's put together a small plan that can help you achieve each goal. What is it you need or who is it you need to meet to accomplish this goal? If you do not personally know this person, write down your 6° of separation for you to meet this person. Write down your barriers. What besides people are stopping you from achieving this goal? I want you to analyze each answer and write down what is stopping you from accomplishing that goal and why. What is important in your life? Why? What is the reason for your having that regret and is there anything you can do to change the feeling of regret?

At the end of this process, you should now have a complete set of goals and a list of barriers that are preventing you from accomplishing these goals. Is it an excuse, fear or true barrier such as knowledge that is keeping you from achieving this goal?

Goal	What or Who	Barrier

In the next few chapters, we will examine barriers and learn how to overcome them.

CHAPTER 5
What are the Barriers that Prevent You from Being Properous

All our dreams can come true – if we have the courage to persue them."

-Walt Disney

Back in 1987 I did a driver's reaction time test with Greyhound Bus Lines. The test worked by the means of a gun that shoots chalk attached to the braking system of the bus. As you are driving along at a defined speed you hear a gun shot that makes a chalk mark on the road. You have to react immediately by pressing the brake pedal which sends the gun off again making another chalk mark on the road. The distance between the two chalk marks divided by the speed determined your reaction time. The times of the people who participate fluctuated between .25 to .4 seconds.

Between saying we want to do a specific task and the excuse "but" popping into our mind, we have approximately 0.3 seconds. It is within that time frame that we can work to change our way of thinking. Maybe slow down, and the next time a decision or choice has to be made, think of the 0.3 second reaction, analyze what led you down the path to that decision. Learning to think before rushing to a decision is a learning process and will not happen over night.

A major barrier to your success will be inner conflict (excuses, fears). You must resolve any inner conflicts you have in order to realize your potential.

You're thinking of change, but...

You've had many years of practice producing excuses or fears. The faster you recognize these buts and re-motivate yourself, the better opportunity you will have to correct the choices you make and improve your decision making prowess. It works like this... I would really like to change the way I am...

> ➤ BUT I'm too tired...
> ➤ BUT I have to look after the kids...
> ➤ BUT golf is on...
> ➤ BUT I don't have time.

These buts are just barriers, the next time you say, but, examine it. Is it an excuse or a realistic but? There are three types of barriers, excuses, fears or actual barriers

An excuse is,
> ➤ I don't have time,
> ➤ I don't have enough money,

A fear is,
> ➤ I might fail, I might get rejected etc.

An actual or true barrier is,
> ➤ I don't know who to ask for help,

> ➢ I don't have the knowledge,
> ➢ I don't have enough resources,
> ➢ I don't know the bylaws etc.

These barriers are easy for you to learn to overcome. You can gain the knowledge by reading or going to school. I don't have enough resources. What do I need? Who can help me?

Exercise 8

Pull out your list from exercise 7 and with two different colors of highlighter let's look at the barriers you have written down. Highlight your excuse or fear with one color and highlight your actual or true barrier with the other color.

The very thing to analyze about your barrier is, is it an excuse or fear, or is it truly something you need additional help with?

Your goal is to connect on an emotional level with your barrier. With each barrier only you can overcome the fear of speaking with or taking action to overcome that barrier. When you truly connect to or take ownership of what is important to you. You exude confidence. If you believe, others will believe. This goes for anything, believe in yourself and your barriers will start to disappear.

The very things that *"press your buttons"* are what give you the knowledge of what needs to improve or grow within you. Things that you dislike about your life can become your greatest teachers in helping you evolve and achieve prosperity. That is why seeing the opportunity for growth in every single situation of your life is the best way to influence that inner you that prevents you from becoming the person you want to be. Learn to love the word "NO," use it as motivation, every time you hear the word "NO," a "YES" is just around the corner. Stop procrastinating, just do what needs to be done.

CHAPTER 6
Examining and Overcoming Excuses and Fears

"You must do the things you think you cannot do."

-Eleanor Roosevelt

Most people are afraid to dream, they would rather reflect on the past. Excuses are the true reason people won't or can't put their dreams on paper. In truth, excuse is another word for fear. It all begins with a commitment to remove the excuses or fears that most of us have placed upon our view of the world and ourselves.

You say to yourself, "I want to achieve…. a certain goal." That little you sitting on your shoulder whispers in your ear.
- But…you can't do that because….,
- You don't have time,
- If you make that call they might say no
- But I have to do this first...
- But I'm too tired...
- But I'm not in the mood...
- But it's just too much to do right now...
- But I'm to inexperienced…

or whatever it might be you say to yourself, that is fear. It could be the fear of success, the fear of failure, the fear of looking silly. It all comes back to the same fear, the fear of rejection. Yes in one way or another we all have the same fear, the fear of rejection.

We all have barriers of some sort, and lives differ whether you are single, a couple, a single parent, have a disability, or are unfortunate to have large outstanding medical bills. There is always a way to change, it is a matter of asking the right people for help and not giving up.

In your notebook, you should now have a list of reasons why you can't accomplish your tasks. Are they excuses or fears or are they true barriers?

How did this little you develop and how can we change your way of operating? In the example below, you see the world and make decisions based on views that others have helped you create over time, whether good or bad, through a filter. The amount of time you have to change your thought processes from the same old often negative thoughts, to an, I can achieve / I will achieve is approximately 0.3 seconds.

Example 1

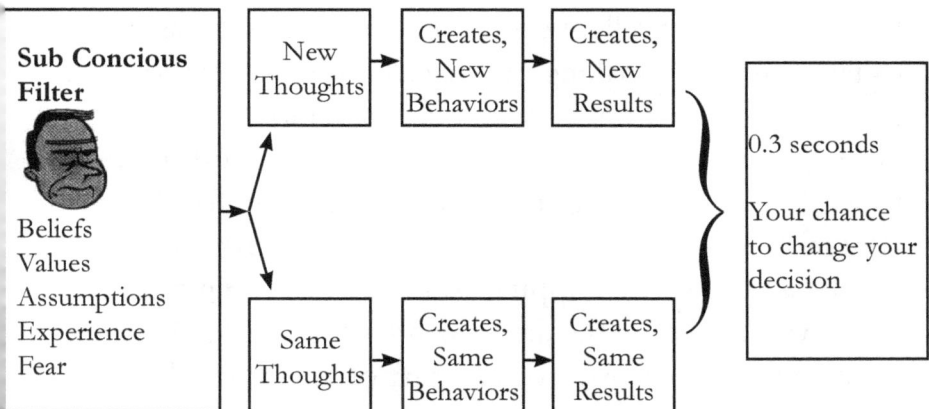

When that little you appears, saying, "but," you need to fight back immediately to rebut each but. In essence, you start to play word games with yourself. Instead of saying but, correct yourself immediately with positive statements. How you talk to yourself is crucial and often a deciding factor in how you feel about yourself. Simply editing yourself is a way to greater achievement and more success.

How often do you wake up in the morning and hit the snooze alarm or say it's too cold I'll stay under the covers for a few more minutes only to regret it later as you sleep in or start running late? Simply get out of bed, get your day started and you will find your day will actually go better. In fact if you get out of bed one hour earlier and let this become your time to do what you want, such as read, meditate, reflect, watch the news or just plan your day, you will begin to feel much better about yourself. It is important to have alone time, it will benefit both yourself and your significant others.

Time is one of the biggest excuses people use so let's look at a typical work week.

After allowing for 56 hours for sleep and 40 hours of work in the schedule there are usually 72 hours of open time. How are you using that time? Going to and from work plus lunch hour are excellent opportunities to learn by listening to tapes, reading, making phone calls or whatever you can do in that time frame. Everyone's situation is different. Sleep patterns and work schedules will vary. From week to week or month to month schedules change for doctors appointments, overtime, extra volunteer work; don't let that be an excuse in stopping you from achieving a goal.

As you can see in the daily calendar I have added soccer, dance, hockey and groceries as part of my schedule and I still have over 60 hours of free time. Everybodies sleep and work patterns will vary. Don't let that be an excuse

Exercise 9

Make a similar calendar for yourself. See how much free time you have. The next time you say "there just doesn't seem to be enough hours in the day", is that really true?

Time	Sunday	Monday	Tuesday	Wednesday	Thursday	Friday	Saturday
12am	Sleep	Sleep	Sleep	Sleep	Sleep	Sleep	Sleep
1am	Sleep	Sleep	Sleep	Sleep	Sleep	Sleep	Sleep
2am	Sleep	Sleep	Sleep	Sleep	Sleep	Sleep	Sleep
3am	Sleep	Sleep	Sleep	Sleep	Sleep	Sleep	Sleep
4am	Sleep	Sleep	Sleep	Sleep	Sleep	Sleep	Sleep
5am	Sleep	Sleep	Sleep	Sleep	Sleep	Sleep	Sleep
6am	Sleep	Sleep	Sleep	Sleep	Sleep	Sleep	Sleep
7am	Sleep	Wake up	Wake up	Wake up	Wake up	Wake up	Sleep
8am	My time	My time	My time	My time	My time	My time	My time
9am		Commute	Commute	Commute	Commute	Commute	
10am		Work	Work	Work	Work	Work	
11am		Work	Work	Work	Work	Work	
12pm		Lunch	Lunch	Lunch	Lunch	Lunch	
1pm		Work	Work	Work	Work	Work	Groceries
2pm		Work	Work	Work	Work	Work	
3pm		Work	Work	Work	Work	Work	
4pm		Work	Work	Work	Work	Work	
5pm		Commute	Commute	Commute	Commute	Commute	
6pm		Soccer					
7pm				Dance			
8pm		Soccer					
9pm					Hockey		
10pm							
11pm							

The best way to release your fear is to feel and embrace it. Stop fighting it. If your fear is a shyness towards people, that is usually a self confidence issue. Be confident in who you are, say "HI" or "GOOD MORNING" to random people you meet on the street. Eventually you will become less shy and hold a more substantial conversation with people you don't know and thus building self confidence at the same time. When you do, your fear will disappear and you will feel utterly amazed. This is your greatest opportunity to grow. Run towards your excuses or fears. Never run away from them.

As each negative comes out, fight back with a positive one. Every time you say to yourself, "but or come up with an excuse" immediately ask yourself , "Why did I say but"? Just do what you are thinking! What is the worst thing that can happen? New positive thoughts create a new behavior that create new results and that's what we're trying to achieve. By refusing to cave in to your excuse or fear you will start to overcome that barrier.

CHAPTER 7
Overcoming Barriers

"Life's up and downs provide windows of opportunity to determine your values and goals. Think of using all obstacles as stepping stones to build the life you want."

-Marsha Sinetar

True barriers

True barriers are usually easier to overcome. However it might be more time consuming.

A true barrier might be as follows:

I want to earn an Undergraduate or Graduate Degree. But I don't have enough money. Here I could ask my employer to help, if they say no, I could see if I can get money from my 401k or RRSP, is there any government financial aid available to me such as Pal Grants, Staffords Loans or OSAP loans.

or

My goal is to open a home for the homeless but I don't have the experience or resources necessary. I can give up or put it on paper and see what it looks like.

1. How many people will my home accommodate?
2. What is the purpose of this home?

3. What size of home is necessary?
4. Where is the home located?
5. What government programs can help me achieve my goal?
6. How can I raise the funds to meet my costs?
   ➤ Fund raise
   ➤ Businesses
   ➤ Friends
   ➤ Government Programs
7. Who are the people in my community that can help make this happen?
8. What bylaws would I have to consider?

Here, I have broken down the barriers into some incremental steps. I will attack each, one at a time. As I gain knowledge in one area, it will give me the confidence to go forth. Small-steps are how to overcome true barriers. Remember what Neil Armstrong said as he put his foot on the moon, "One small step for man, one giant leap for mankind."

When making a decision, one of two things may happen. I make an impulse decision, or I analyze should I / shouldn't I. In some cases decisions are over thought which can have an affect opposite to what you were contemplating.

Example 2

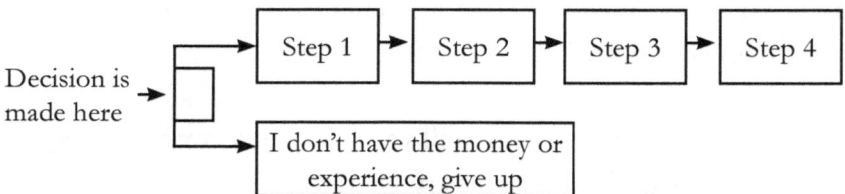

I have two choices, give up because I don't have the experience or at least try. Think, even if you try and fail at least you will never regret not having tried at all.

One of the greatest tools available to us is to tell as many people as we can what we are trying to achieve. The pressure of many people knowing will give us the motivation to keep going forward and finding ways to overcome barriers that might be prohibiting our successful completion of a task or goal. Depending on the goal, some people may be negative, guess what? We just found out who are not our friends.

A real friend or mentor would encourage, offer to help where necessary or highlight some of the challenges we may face and wish us good luck.

Why would someone we consider a good friend react in a negatively to our comments on our goals or aspirations.

➤ Jealousy
➤ We may become more successful than them
➤ We may accomplish something and find new friends

Who knows, who cares, find new friends with positive outlooks on life. We attract who we are, if we are negative in nature, so are the people we surround ourselves with.

If we become a person who believes "I can accomplish anything," we begin to attract positive people into our life.

CHAPTER 8
Creating Your Plan for Prosperity and Financial Peace

"No bird soars too high if he soars with his own wings"
-William Blake

Now we know more about who we are as a person and understand some of our weakness, the time has come to create our plan on how to achieve prosperity and financial peace?

We as a society generally proceed through the financial stages of our lives in the same manner. From 20 – 39 we spend most of our time worrying about cash flow. This age group spends most of their money paying bills and taking care of the basics and whatever is left over goes to material possessions such as ipods, cars, stereos etc. Between 40 -59 we are primarily concerned with asset accumulation, minimizing taxes, diversifying our investments to protect ourselves. People in this group aren't retired yet, but they need to grow their capital in order to retire comfortably and send their kids to university or college. Ages 60 and older are mostly concerned with asset management. Protect what they have accumulated and utilize it in a manner that will preserve capital so they don't run out of money in their later years of retirement.

They become more concerned about the estate or legacy they will leave behind.

Exercise 10

First, let's prioritize. Find or create a 12 month calendar. Look at your list of goals and number them accordingly, number 1 being the most important goal you would like to achieve or if you like, the easiest for you to achieve. Success will keep you moving forward. On your calendar place as much information as possible about your current schedule, work, PTA, kids soccer, swimming, what ever it is in your daily life that needs to be on your calendar.

Now for your number one goal, place your start date in the calendar. What steps need to be taken to complete this task, and what costs are associated with the task? Write down in the calendar, when you will have completed this task. Do this for each goal and task within a goal, and you will now have a timetable in place to accomplish prosperity and financial peace.

Do not over task yourself or you will just quit. Make the timetable something you can keep both emotionally and financially. Take small steps, it is less frustrating and easier to backtrack if necessary.

Listed below are some typical goals, however fill in your own.

Goals and Concerns

Current will up to date as of _____

Living wills completed as of _____

The first two, your will and living will are mandatory and should be completed immediately. No matter your age, you are never too young.

___ Start a savings plan
___ Start a new business
___ Have a vacation

Volunteering
___ Charity Work
___ Coaching

Retirement Planning
___ Retire early and comfortably
___ Ensure my funds last through retirement

Saving for a major purchase
___ Purchase Cottage/Investment property
___ Leisure activities (travel, buy an RV, etc.)
___ opening a business

Education Planning
___ Pay for my childs/grandchilds education
___ Pay to upgrade my education

Tax Planning
___ Reduce my income taxes

Estate Planning
___ Preserve my estate for my beneficiaries
___ Estate Tax Planning
___ Final Expenses

Other

—

—

—

CHAPTER 9
Cash Flow Analysis

"When I hear somebody sigh, Life is Hard, I am always tempted to ask, Compared to what?"

-Sydney Harris

Make a few photocopies of this exercise, complete in pencil, as you should re-evaluate this once a year.

In this exercise you are going to your analyze your debts and income.

How much cash will you need? Identify your insurance needs. If your spouse dies do you have enough life insurance to meet child care needs, pay off the mortgage and eat? Do you have disability insurance? Will it cover your obligations? Identify your retirement needs. How much of a pension will you have when you retire? One in three people will become disabled for 90 days or more once in their lifetime prior to the age of 65. Do you have a nest egg?

Learn about your finances. Don't just sign your tax return.

To understand you finances you are going to complete a cash flow analysis. To help you along I have listed the meanings of some of the terminology on the Income items necessary. All the other items are self explanatory.

Net Monthly Income = your gross monthly income minus any taxes or deductions.

Salary = is the amount you earn for the job you do or services you provide.

Self Employed Income = income you make from your business.

Dividend/Interest/Capital Gains = income you make from investments,

Rents / Annuities = payments made to you for renting a room, apartment, house, cottage or payments from an insurance company investment.

Pension/OAS/CPP = income from registered retirement accounts such as 401k, Investment Retirement Account (IRA), RRSP, RRIF LRIF, Old Age Security, Company pension, Canada Pension Plan, Other countries Pension Plans that you qualify for.

Bonus/Gifts/ Miscellaneous Income = income paid as a bonus or money given to you as a gift, inheritance or trust etc.

Alimony/Child Support = money paid to you from a former spouse or partner.

Other = any money given to you from other sources not listed.

The rest are fairly self explanatory.

Exercise 11
Cash Flow Analysis
NET MONTHLY INCOME (gross minus any taxes or deductions)

Salaries	_____
Self Employed	_____
Dividend/Interest	_____
Capital Gains	_____
RRIF/IRA	_____
Rents/Annuities	_____
Pension/CPP/OAS	_____
Bonus/Gifts/ Misc. Inc.	_____
Alimony/Child Support	_____
Other	_____
TOTAL NET INCOME	$_____

EXPENSES all expense are in italic
REGULAR MONTHLY SAVINGS

Registered Savings	_____
Non-Registered Savings	_____
Investment	_____
Other	_____
Total Current Savings	$_____

DEBTS

Mortgage(s)	_____
Line of Credit	_____
Credit Cards	_____
Leverage Loan	_____

Car Loans _____
School Loan _____
Consolidation Debts _____
Other _____
Total Debt Payments $_____

HOME
Rent _____
Property Taxes _____
Insurance _____
Utilities _____
Phone _____
Cell Phone/Internet _____
Repairs/Maintenance _____
Total Home $_____

TRANSPORTATION
Gas _____
Insurance _____
Repairs/Parking _____
Other _____
Total Transportation $_____

INSURANCE PREMIUMS
Life _____
Disability _____
Health/Dental _____
Critical Illness _____
Other _____
Total Insurance $_____

DIRECT MEDICAL/DENTAL
Glasses/Prescriptions _____

Dental _____

Other _____

Total Health $_____

FLEXIBLE FAMILY NEEDS
Clothing _____

Groceries _____

Restaurants/Lunches _____

Tim Horton's/Starbucks _____

Vacations/Holidays _____

Entertainment _____

Education/Tuition _____

Hair/Cosmetics _____

Child Care _____

Subscriptions _____

Tobacco/Alcohol _____

Hobbies (golf, skiing, etc.) _____

Other (gifts, charity, etc.) _____

Total Family Needs $_____

TOTAL INCOME $_____

TOTAL EXPENSES $_____

UNCOMMITTED INCOME (INCOME - EXPENSES)

$_____

AMOUNT WILLING TO COMMIT TO GOALS

$_____

Chapter 10
Finding Extra Money

"Without a struggle, there can be no progress."
-Frederick Douglass

After the last exercise, you now have a number called uncommitted income. This is the number you want to analyze and try to increase. Look at your budget. Is there any waste or monies that could be put to better use elsewhere?

For 1 week keep a journal of where and what you spend money on.

Example 3

Every morning you stop in at Starbucks or Tim Horton's to purchase a coffee and a bagel. How much does it cost? Let's say $2.80 a day times five days equal $14.00, and then times 50 weeks equals $700. This is an approximate amount of how much you spend on coffee and a bagel every morning over the course of the year. Imagine if you do that two or three times a day. Is there an opportunity to save money?

$700 a year over twenty years invested at an 8% annual rate of return would add approximately $32,033 to your retirement or future goals.

Example 4

You smoke one pack of cigarettes a day $9.14 times seven days equals $64 a week, times again by 52 weeks equals $3,328 a year. $3,328 a year invested over 20 years at 8% rate of return would have accumulated approximately $152,296. Look how much you could have saved just by cutting down to one half pack a day or quitting.

The numbers in the last two examples over a five year period could have been a nice down payment for a small home, boat, child's education or whatever your goals may be.

Exercise 12

Analyze your budget, be true, or it won't work. Where can you save money? You should now have a true uncommitted income. It is imperative you do this exercise once per year because as you correct old spending habits, new habits arise and bite you in the butt.

Chapter 11
Balance Sheet

"Seize the day and put the least possible trust in tomorrow."

-Horace

In order to plan for financial peace you need to know where you are today. This next exercise will give you the opportunity to get a clear financial picture of your current status and what needs to be changed.

Exercise 13

Make a number of photocopies of this exercise, fill the numbers in pencil as accurately as possible. Then, transcribed the Total Assets, Total Liabilities and Net Worth numbers to the chart at the back of the book.

Balance Sheet
ASSETS LIABILITIES

Home	_____	Mortgage	_____
Cottage	_____	Credit Line	_____
Real Estate	_____	Auto Loan	_____
Car	_____	Other Loans	_____
Investments	_____	Credit Cards	_____
IRA/RRSP/401(k)	_____	Other Debts	_____
Other Assets	_____	Leverage Loans	_____
TOTAL ASSETS	_____	- TOTAL LIABILITIES	_____
NET WORTH	_____		

Your net worth is what you are worth today. Obviously you want this number to be larger every year.

Your net worth could have drastic swings in value depending on investment values, interest rates or property values. So if you have a large increase or decrease from year to year, its not always good news or bad. Know the number that makes up your net worth.

CHAPTER 12
Creating Your Financial Plan

"You must be the change you wish to see in the world."

-Gandhi

Once you have identified your goals and concerns, it is sometimes better to turn your financial planning objectives over to an experienced financial planner.

Some people have no interest in dealing with their personal finances. They know little about money and find the subject matter boring and uninteresting. To deal with money matters when you haven't the time or interest becomes a daunting task. However, it is still important for you to learn the language of investing and to understand your objectives and risk tolerance. Ask your friends, who they use. Just because a financial planner has some letters behind his/her name does not necessarily mean that he/she is the best financial planner for you. Interview for this position as you would interview for hiring a new employee.

Financial Advisors work in many ways, some will charge you a flat rate for a financial plan, others won't hoping to get all your business and make their money off of your investments. They may charge an upfront fee on the amount you invest or take a commission from the investment company the investments are held with, in which you may have to pay a penalty if you liquidate early

Example 5

Flat fee – you find a Financial Advisor and ask him/her for help. They may charge you $1000 for the financial plan and make money on your investments if you invest with him/her.

Front end fee – you give an advisors $10,000 to invest. The advisor will take a set amount from the $10,000 before he/she invests the money. So at a 5% front end fee, he/she will invest $9,500 and the other $500 is the fee. Usually when this is done you can liquidate your investments at market value with no penalty.

Back end – you give your advisor $10,000, he/she send the check to the investment company investing all $10,000. He/she is paid a commission from the company. To ensure the company earns the commission that they paid on your behalf, they may lock your investments for a period of time usually, seven years. This does not mean you can not liquidate the investments at market value at any time. It means that you will pay a penalty if you do liquidate your investments. The penalty depends how long the investments were held. The penalty usually reduces 1% per year until it reaches zero.

If you are dealing with stocks or bonds you will usually pay a percentage of the value invested for each trade, although many trading companies have started charging a flat fee per trade.

In most situations the advisor will also earn what is called an annual trailer fee on the investments. Trailer fees vary with each investment. As your investments go up, the advisor makes more money on the trailer fee, conversely if they go down the advisor will make less.

Ask questions such as, how do you get paid? What is your investment philosophy? What is your experience? Don't let a lot of letters behind the name (CFP, CA, CPA, CGA) confuse you. Just because they have these designations, does not necessarily mean they are good advisors.

The components of your financial plan are as follows:
- Accomplish set goals
- Investment planning.
- Tax planning.
- Children's education.
- Insurance planning.
- Retirement planning
- Estate planning.

Let's look at each one independently.

Financial Planning

Many people live from day to day, paycheck to paycheck. Unfortunately they also spend from day-to-day and never get a chance to build a financial nest egg. To make progress in starting to create your retirement plan, saving for a new home or a new car, you are better to start off in small steps or you will be frustrated and give up. List your goals in terms of 1 year, 5 year and 10 year goals.

In order to achieve any financial goals you are going to have to learn to pay yourselves first, before any bills. Your bills will be paid, it will all come together, you will see. Set up a savings account, determine what your hourly wage is and pay the first hour of every day to yourself. Is it too much to ask, that for all your hard work, you get to keep the wage for the first hour of every day you work. You will be amazed at how fast you will begin to accumulate a financial nest egg to help achieve your goals.

When creating a financial plan the uncertainty of future prices and inflation creates a large dilemma in planning for the future. The best we can do is estimate future cost based on current costs. If inflation averages 3% it will take approximately 24 years for the price of an item to double.

Investment Planning.

When investing, there are two emotions that drive people's thoughts. One is Fear and the other is Greed. Volatile markets can be risky enough; do not take further risk by getting greedy. Forget about pursuing a hot stock tip or chasing the latest IPO or the number one mutual fund out this past year. Once you have put together a concise plan, let it do its job for you. If you are already retired during volatile times, it is important that you stay liquid. A good rule of thumb for investing is to take a look at your age. If you take 100 minus your age, that will give you the breakdown for what should be in equities and what should be in fixed income or liquid type assets. As an example, if you are 55 years of age, you would want to be sure 55% of your portfolio is invested in fixed income type investments and 45% of your portfolio could then be invested in conservative style equity or dividend style funds. When you are younger you can afford to be in all equities. However as you get to the other side of 50 it is important to start to become less aggressive and start thinking of your actual retirement date. When you are retired, you still need to have your portfolio grow to ensure you don't run out of money in the future.

Equities are classed as Stocks, or Mutual Funds and Income Trust that hold various Stocks that create a capital gain or dividend.

Fixed Income investments usually generate an interest income such as Bonds, Bond Funds, Money Market Funds, Mortgage Funds or Bank Accounts to name a few.

Asset allocation or how you decide to divide your money among the different types of investments is the most important decision you will make.

Studies show that 92% of your investment return depends on the way you allocate your money among different types of investments. And only 8% of your success depends on the actual type of investment itself.

In this section, I am going to take you through the steps involved in putting an investment plan together using mutual funds. This process is a typical process that we as a Financial Advisors use with 80% of our clients.

To be truthful, at the end of the day a mutual fund is a mutual fund is a mutual fund. It does not matter what institution or family of funds holds the investment, most mutual funds in a given sector will usually perform to within 1 to 2% of each other over a 15 to 20 year period. This applies to equity funds, bond funds, dividend funds and other fixed income funds. Most mutual funds run in a cycle where two out of every five years the fund will be down in value over the previous year. Unfortunately we never know the cycle, whether it will be the first and second year, second and fourth, third and fifth. If you look historically at a year to year annual return for a period of ten to fifteen years, you will see how this cycle develops every five years. If we knew the exact cycle nobody would ever lose money.

One of the most important factors of asset allocation is to regularly re-balance your portfolio to its original structure that you had previously set up. As an example, let's say, you invested 70% in equities, 20% in dividends and 10% in bonds. Your portfolio grew, however the equities grew at a higher rate and the balance changed to 80% equities, 12% bonds and 8% dividends. Unless your risk tolerance has changed, you would want to rebalance your portfolio back to its original format of 70% equities, 20% dividends and 10 % bonds. Yes that means liquidating some of your positions and purchasing other investments that might not have done as well as equities, but you have a plan and you would want to keep that structure in place. This is where most people make their biggest mistake as the greed factor sets in and they begin to invest outside their risk tolerance looking to make the quick buck. What goes up can come down just as fast. Therefore, it is worth it to look at the percentages held in each category and keep this in place going forward.

The first step in putting together a financial plan after knowing your goals and concerns is to know what type of investor you are. The first question many people ask is "Do I have enough money for a financial plan?" Whenever you are planning to invest money you should have a plan. Money should always be invested under the guise of what type of investor you are, whether it is conservative, moderate or aggressive and the time frame as to when you will need to liquidate or redeem that investment.

As a guideline, any investment that needs to be redeemed

or liquidated within a 5 year period should be invested in a conservative form of investment, such as a high interest savings account, a bond fund, a Guaranteed Investment Certificate (GIC), Money Market Account or Mortgage Backed Securities.

When investing for a 5 to 8 year period of time, a more moderate type of investment can be considered such as a dividend fund, bond funds or a conservative equity fund.

When investing for a period of time greater than eight years you may pick a different form or more aggressive type of investment such as aggressive equity funds, sector funds or hedge funds to name a few. Sector funds are funds that specialize in a certain sector such as financial services, health and science or high-tech. Over the past few years, high-tech funds have established a bad name for losing money when the high-tech bubble burst. However, look at how much technology plays a part in your life today. By no means are technology funds dead, you just need to invest in a wise manner.

When investing in a high tech or a sector fund, you should never invest more than 10% of your portfolio in any given sector.

Exercise 14
By answering the following asset allocation questionnaire, this will give you an idea of what type of investor you are, whether it is conservative, moderate, or aggressive. Before you begin investing a more thorough risk analysis will be done by your advisor. This is to be used as an example only.

A. Indicate the statement that most closely describes your approach to inflation

1 ❑ To attempt to keep pace with inflation, I am willing to take on a low level of fluctuation in the value of my investments.

3 ❑ I am willing to take a moderate level of fluctuation in the value of my investments so that my investment returns can be expected to be somewhat higher than the level of inflation over the long run.

5 ❑ I am willing to take on a high level of fluctuation in the value of my investments so my investment return can be expected to be significantly higher that the level of inflation over the long run.

B. When will you start to withdraw money from your investments?

1 ❑ 2 - 3 years
2 ❑ 4 - 5 years
3 ❑ 6 -10 years
4 ❑ 10 - 15 years
5 ❑ Over 15 years

Once you begin, how and when do you anticipate withdrawing money from your portfolio

1 ❑ Lump sum
0 ❑ Less than 2 years
2 ❑ 2-5 years
3 ❑ 6-10 years
5 ❑ 11-15 years
6 ❑ Over 15 years

C. Select the investment you would be most likely to choose. Suppose you have $20,000 to invest, and you have only the two investment options below, the anticipated returns of each investment after one year are.

5 ❑ Investment A: 70% chance of gaining $2,000
    30% chance of losing $800
3 ❑ Investment B: 100% chance of gaining $750

D. Let's say that the return on an investment equity mutual fund has been averaging 8% per year for the last 5 years. At the end of last year, however, your fund experienced a decline of 12%, which is similar to other funds with the same objective. What would you do at this point?

10 ❑ I would buy more of the investment
6 ❑ I would hold my investment
4 ❑ I would sell some of the investment
0 ❑ I would sell all the investment

Total your score by adding together the numbers beside the answer you have chosen and place yourself into one of the categories below.
♦ under 5 – conservative
♦ 6 – 14 – Moderate conservative
♦ 15-20 – Moderate
♦ 21-25 – Moderate Aggressive
♦ Over 25 – Aggressive

You have now identified the type of investor you are, in your notebook take a look at the investments you currently have or the amount of money you are going to start investing. Below you will find a list of asset allocation charts and how you should diversify your money among these funds. Compare your current investments with the charts. These charts are only a guideline for you to use, you should seek the help of a professional when investing your money.

Let's say you have $100,000. Look in the conservative portfolio and your real property fund should have 7% of that money or $7000. Your government bond funds should have 27% or $27000, and so on down the list until you have completed the entire amount of $100,000. Now looking at the $27,000, for the Government bond you can break that equally into different fund families should you want further diversification. Just be sure each company is not holding the same investment as the other in their mutual fund. Some commonality is O.K, but at least 70% of the portfolio should be held in different bonds or stocks. Keep in mind the more fund families you use the more paperwork you will have and the harder it is to track. A fund family is the company that owns the mutual fund.

You can achieve diversification simply by using what is known as a fund of funds portfolio. Simply choose your risk tolerance, conservative, moderate, aggressive and invest in the appropriate fund of funds portfolio.

You now have a diversified investment plan. Congratulations!

The following charts on the next few pages are only a guide to show how to diversify your funds. Before investing you should seek the advice of a professional in this area to help set up your plan.

CDN = Canadian

US = United States
Gov't = Government
Corp = Corporate
LC = Large Cap

Conservative Model	
Asset Class	Asset Class %
Cash	20
Fixed Income	60
Equity	20
Fixed	
Real Property	7
Gov't Bonds	27
Corp Bonds	26
Total Fixed	60
Money Market	20
Total Cash	
Cdn Balanced	
Cdn LC Growth	2
Cdn LC Value	3
Cdn Small Cap	
US Balanced	
US LC Growth	3
US LC Value	5
US Small Cap	
Europe	4
Japan	
Emerging Markets	
Global LC Growth	1
Global LC Value	2
Asian/Pacific	

Conservative Moderate Model	
Asset Class	Asset Class %
Cash	10
Fixed Income	45
Equity	45
Fixed	
Real Property	4
Gov't Bonds	21
Corp Bonds	20
Total Fixed	45
Money Market	10
Total Cash	
Cdn Balanced	
Cdn LC Growth	3
Cdn LC Value	4
Cdn Small Cap	2
US Balanced	
US LC Growth	6
US LC Value	11
US Small Cap	3
Europe	10
Japan	
Emerging Markets	
Global LC Growth	2
Global LC Value	4
Asian/Pacific	

Moderate Model	
Asset Class	Asset Class %
Cash	0
Fixed Income	37
Equity	63
Foreign Fixed	
Real Property	3
Gov't Bonds	17
Corp Bonds	17
Total Fixed	37
Money Market	0
Total Cash	
Cdn Balanced	0
Cdn LC Growth	3
Cdn LC Value	6
Cdn Small Cap	3
US Balanced	
US LC Growth	7
US LC Value	12
US Small Cap	3
Europe	14
Japan	4
Emerging Markets	
Global LC Growth	4
Global LC Value	5
Asian/Pacific	
Asian/Pacific	

Moderate Aggressive	
Asset Class	Asset Class %
Cash	0
Fixed Income	15
Equity	85
Foreign Fixed	
Real Property	
Gov't Bonds	7
Corp Bonds	8
Total Fixed	15
Money Market	0
Total Cash	
Cdn Balanced	0
Cdn LC Growth	5
Cdn LC Value	7
Cdn Small Cap	5
US Balanced	
US LC Growth	12
US LC Value	17
US Small Cap	5
Europe	14
Japan	5
Emerging Markets	3
Global LC Growth	5
Global LC Value	7
Asian/Pacific	
Asian/Pacific	

Aggressive Model	
Asset Class	Asset Class %
Cash	0
Fixed Income	0
Equity	100
Foreign Fixed	
Real Property	0
Gov't Bonds	0
Corp Bonds	0
Total Fixed	0
Money Market	0
Total Cash	
Cdn Balanced	0
Cdn LC Growth	5
Cdn LC Value	9
Cdn Small Cap	3
US Balanced	
US LC Growth	14
US LC Value	18
US Small Cap	4
Europe	16
Japan	6
Emerging Markets	7
Global LC Growth	6
Global LC Value	9
Asian/Pacific	3
Asian/Pacific	

Tax Planning

It is imperative that you take advantage of your tax code. Everyone has to pay their fair share of taxes. People look for so-called tax loopholes. Trust me, there is no such thing as a loophole. The government has designed the tax code with tax deductions, if you qualify for them. The rich and famous take advantage of every deduction possible. They have to, so should you. A simple tip for tax planning is to make sure your investments are invested in the most tax advantaged way, an example of this would be to make sure your investments pay dividends or capital gains in order to get the capital gain exemption if available or the dividend tax credit if available. An example of a dividend is, you purchase a bank preferred stock (share) for $10, every three months you may receive a dividend payment of 25 cents for each share you own. Now if you sell that same stock for $12.50, you have a gain of $2.50 also known as a capital gain. If instead you sold the stock for $8.50 you would have a $1.50 capital loss. Investing in typical interest bearing investments will only create a higher tax burden for you. Use tax deferred investment opportunities whenever possible. This is where working with an experienced Financial Advisor to help you in your tax planning endeavors is worth its weight in gold.

Children's Education

Today in 2008, if a child is living at home, while attending college or university, the average education will cost anywhere from $7000-$11000 per year. If your child decides to live in residence his/her education skyrockets to $22,000 to $70,000 per year depending on the school they decide to attend.

For example, my daughter goes to University in Belmont, California. Her tuition fee for 2004 is $24,360. Her room and board totals $12,000 per year. Her books are $2000 a year and her medical fee is $750 per year. This cost is an average cost for there are some less expensive and there are many more expensive universities.

To find the cost of tuition for a college or university today is easy. All you do is go to the schools website and look under tuitions. All the information on you need to know on expenses is there.

Take advantage of your government's education savings plans whenever possible. Investments for these plans are offered by many different Mutual Fund, Insurance Companies or Education Scholarship Organizations. Beware of Education Scholarship Organizations or also known as pooled scholarship plans as they can be very expensive when removing money for an education or if you try to get out of the plan early. When investing for two or more children, if there is a gap of 4 years or more, have separate plans for each. Family plans are a great tool if the children are close in age. If the ages differ by more than 4 years, there is a different investment strategy that is needed for each child. As the older child begins to withdraw from the account, the investments needs to be invested in a more conservative structure than a child that still has 4 years of growth opportunity left. Learn about Education Plans, they are there to help you.

Insurance Planning.

Insurance planning is an integral part of any financial plan. Insurance is used mainly for four reasons.

1. To pay off a mortgage and replace income should a

spouse pass away.
2. To pay for final expenses.
3. Asset protection
4. Wealth Accumulation

There are three basic types of life insurance; term, whole life and universal life. Term insurance is as it sounds, it has a specific time frame or term to expiry, usually at age certain age. When purchasing term insurance only, purchase convertible and renewable because at some point in the future you might decide to keep the insurance on a permanent basis and let your children or beneficiaries pay the premium.

Whole life and Universal life are both permanent insurance policies and are somewhat similar as they both can have a cash value option in the policy. With universal life you have an opportunity to use this policy for asset protection and wealth accumulation and as a tax sheltered account to shelter income you cannot invest in a IRA / 401(k) or RRSP.

As each company has their own set of guidelines for universal and whole policies, many of them are quite complex. You are better to seek the advice of a life insurance representative to explain the options to you directly as there are complicated calculations involved in finding the minimum amount you need to contribute and the maximum that you are allowed.

It is important for you to decide how much life insurance is the correct amount for you. Should you be purchasing insurance to replace a spouse's income, you need to think of investing the proceeds from a payout into a conservative type investment expecting an annual rate of return on average of 6%. Therefore, should you have to replace a $100,000 a year income you would need approximately $1,660,000 in life insurance. Should you have group benefits through your employer you generally have one to two times your annual salary in life insurance. You now need to purchase the rest through a life insurance representative. In most cases life insurance is needed until your children have finished their education and your mortgage has been paid off.

The following are two situations involving families I know personally.

1. In 2004, Robert a forty-two year old married father of two children, Samantha 12 and Cody 14, died of heart failure as a result of diabetes. He was self-employed and quite successful but unfortunately had no will or life insurance in place before he was diagnosed with diabetes. Also, he had no disaster recovery plan in place for the business. His wife was left with a company she had no idea how to run and that had acquired a huge personal debt for landscaping equipment needed for the business, a house with a small mortgage that was not insured, only a part-time job working from 8pm until 2am and a small savings account that will probably last her just over a year.

Last I heard Samantha and Cody had to give up sports, drop out of hockey and their mother was on the verge of bankruptcy.

2. Scott a 35 year old widowed father of two girls Sara 2, Haley 4 and step-father to 16 year-old Jason whose mother Scott had married less than a year ago. Scott had an investment account valued over $400,000 that he inherited

from his parents. Scott had always said, when he had time he would turn that account into a trust for his two girls. Unfortunately on an April morning in 2002 while walking his dog, Scott stepped off a curb and was hit and killed by a car. Scott had no will, a small life insurance policy at one times his salary where he had named Sara and Haley as the beneficiaries.

Paul, Scott's brother had a two year battle in court trying to recover most of the $400,000 for Sara and Haley who now live with Paul and his wife. It cost Paul $15,000 in legal fees.

Both situations could have been avoided just by having a will and doing some life insurance and estate planning.

Beware of some of the traps that are set when purchasing mortgage insurance. In many cases when a bank sells you mortgage insurance, it is only creditor insurance and most mortgage or creditor insurance policies require a medical be done after the passing of the client before the money is released. This is a clear way that insurance companies are able to refuse to pay their claims should a medical condition not have been disclosed or discovered previously. With typical mortgage insurance you purchase from your bank, the bank is the beneficiary and is used to pay off only the amount outstanding on your mortgage regardless of the wishes or circumstances of your dependants. This does not however pay off early payout penalties which can amount to thousands of dollars. The policy can also be cancelled by the bank or the issuing company when you renegotiate your mortgage. So if you develop an illness such as diabetes you may not qualify for insurance the next time you re-negotiate your mortgage.

Here is an example of how to set up a life insurance policy to replace a $100,000 a year income presuming there is no insurance elsewhere. Purchase a $25,000 Universal Life policy with level premiums, then, add a 20 year term renewable and convertible rider for $1,635,000. At the end of the 20 years you now have the opportunity to cancel the term rider should this insurance no longer be necessary; however you can keep the $25,000 in force for your final expenses.

Besides the term of the insurance policy, the next question is, should it be a single policy, multi-life, joint-first-to-die or joint last-to-die? A single policy is as it sounds, to cover one person.

Many times when someone purchases mortgage insurance the banks will sell them a joint-first-to-die. The problem with this type of policy is when you have an accident and both you and your spouse are killed. If one of you hangs on to life for 60 to 90 days and then passes away the policy will only pay for one death. A better way is to purchase you're your life policy for your mortgage and structure the policy to use a multi-life policy as it is one policy, which covers multiple lives and generally cost no more than $5 a month extra. A joint-last-to-die policy is a good policy to use should one person have health issues or you are using it as an estate planning tool to cover tax liabilities upon the death of the last surviving spouse.

As you can see, once you have decided on the amount of insurance needed, you are better advised to sit down with a representative, rather than trying to buy it yourself over the internet because of the complexities of the insurance policies and the companies that sell them.

Retirement Planning

To have an effective retirement plan you need to know what income opportunities are available to you when you retire. Income opportunities can be help from government agencies such as Old Age Security or income from Annuities, Income Supplements, a pension from your company that you previously worked for, money that you have saved in your government sponsored plans such as 401(k), IRA or RRSP or other investments that you have accumulated over your lifetime. It is also important for you to know what it is you want to do when you retire, travel, move to the cottage, golf. What ever it is, you need to know how much it is going to cost you so you can start saving now.

Estate Planning

Frequently, poor estate planning leads to family battles and it often causes or allows the deceased's wishes to be ignored. In addition, probate procedures are all made public, causing family privacy to be lost. Sit your beneficiaries down and let them know what the terms of your will are. Ask them what they would like. As an example, you have a cottage that will be left to your children. However, there could be some capital gains tax when you and your spouse have passed away. Not all your children might want to participate in the cottage and would prefer to take something else from the estate instead. Yes, it can be uncomfortable, but at least you know when you have passed away there will be no fighting and your last wishes will be respected.

The following is a list of terms some necessary for you to understand when creating an estate plan with your attorney:

Estate. All of the property owned by an individual prior to the distribution of that property under the terms of a will, trust or inheritance laws. An individual's estate includes all assets and liabilities. Bank accounts are included as assets.

Property. Property is described as either real or personal. Real property is real estate, and personal property is everything else. Personal property includes physical assets such as automobiles, equipment, household items, etc. Personal property also includes financial property, such as securities, notes or loans receivable, bank accounts, cash, insurance policies, 401(k), IRA and RRSP's.

What happens should you Die Intestate. We need to do estate planning to avoid dying "intestate". Dying intestate means dying without creating either a will, or a trust which provides instructions for passing your estate on to your heirs. If you do not have a will or trust then probate, creditors, lawsuits, judgments, lawyers, and estate or death taxes can erode much if not all of the value of your estate.

The inheritance laws (laws of intestacy) of your government will determine how your property will be passed to your heirs should you die without a will or a trust. If you have no heirs that fit the government's formula, the assets will then be taken by the government.

Problems with Probate. If you die with any property titled in your personal name, there must be a probate process for that property if the estate is above a minimum size. Probate is the government's legal procedure for handling some major functions for your estate. Having a will drawn up in advance of your death will take care of the identification of the rightful heirs and their share. With no valid will for your estate the government will use its own formula for determining who the heirs are and their share. Even with a will, the re-titling of your property still must be handled through a court administered probate procedure.

You want to avoid probate is when because it can be an emotional, expensive and time consuming process. In some cases probate ends up in litigation that drags on for many years.

One way to avoid probate is by using a family estate planning trust, either a living trust or a life estate trust.

Problem's due to no Living Will. When a property owner has either sole or joint tenancy ownership and then becomes mentally incapacitated the property is in legal limbo. This is due to the incapacitated owner being incapable of conveying legal title or signing legally binding documents. This can prevent the property from being sold or even being leased. Often times an expensive and time delaying court procedure is the only answer. A family trust is the most comprehensive and best detailed manner to deal with incapacitation issues. But, a simple device known as a durable power of attorney will also take care of the problem in some cases. Sometimes, these Power of Attorneys are known as a Financial Power of Attorney and Health and Welfare Power of Attorney.

Protecting your estate from divorce and lawsuits. The lack of a formal estate plan leaves the estate owner extremely vulnerable on this issue. This topic is known simply as "asset protection". The use of a special type family trust is one of the best ways to achieve asset protection.

What Is a Trust? Some family estate plan functions that trusts are required for are:

1. Control the transfer of estate to the proper heirs
2. Management of the estate during mental incapacitation
3. Reduction or elimination of estate or death taxation
4. Protecting the estate from lawsuits
5. Probate avoidance

A trust is a legal entity used in special ways to take care of property. Trusts are a legal agreement between two parties. These parties are known as the grantor and the trustee. The grantor and trustee create the agreement for the benefit of a third party known as the beneficiary. Private agreements have tremendous flexibility in their provisions. Even though a trust is a private agreement, it is accepted in the courts and by law as an independent legal entity. In fact, trusts are independent entities very much like corporations. Through their trustee they may own property, they may have to file tax returns and pay taxes. They may own bank and investment accounts, earn income, distribute profits to the beneficiaries, conduct business activities, etc.

A Grantor is an individual who may own properties which he/she wishes to have managed, controlled, protected and transferred to heirs by a trust. Once the property is in the trust, the grantor no longer holds the legal title to the property, though they usually retain the exclusive rights to use the property or its income and usually retain full control of the property. The trustee is the legal administrator of the trust and the legal title holder of the property. The grantors' relationship to the trust is determined by the language which they put into the trust agreement. The beneficiaries are the individuals or charities that receive benefits or income from the trust property and eventually receive the property itself. A Grantor may retain for his/her lifetime the rights to the income and use of the trust property and then the beneficiaries will receive their benefits after the grantor dies. In still other cases the grantor and beneficiaries may both receive benefits from the trust simultaneously.

Now that you have your plan in place, it is time to allocate your uncommitted income. Take 20% of that uncommitted income and put it into a fund called an emergency fund. This fund needs to be the value of three months of your total salary. Once you have achieved your emergency fund you can now allocate that money to another goal. Take 40% of your uncommitted income and put this in your most important goal fund. Take 20% of the uncommitted income, and that becomes your fund for accomplishing your other goals. Now the remaining 20% goes to your retirement plan. Using the knowledge you have gain investing as you achieve one goal you can start to move money around to help you accomplish other goals.

Chapter 13
What Will My Retirement Look Like

"Within you is the divine capacity to manifest and attract all that you need or desire."

-Wayne Dyer

During this chapter it is important to remember you are using today's dollar values.

Demographic imbalance will start to play havoc with our pension systems and public support programs provided by our governments over the next few decades as people born between 1947 and 1966 begin to retire. By the time the bulk of the Baby Boomers reach retirement there will not be enough working people from the baby boomer period to fund our pension and public programs. Therefore, you must anticipate that the personal financial costs will be far greater than it was for your parents.

When setting goals for your retirement it is important to try and look into the future to see what your life will look like if you achieve your goals. What is the size of your home? Have you downsized? Usually our biggest asset next to our income is our home and many people forget to use this in the planning stages. Take a look at the value of your home. When it is paid off and you downsize, how much will you have left over after purchasing your new home?

An important fact to remember is that over the next 10 – 15 years the value of large single detached homes will start to drop in value as more and more baby boomers downsize and move into semis, townhouses or condos. Single level semis and condos will start to increase in value. You can already see the trend happening with condos and semis in many major cities.

Unfortunately there are more of us baby boomers than there are younger people, who are able to buy the big $500,000 and up homes to sustain those values. Therefore when it comes time for you to sell, the dollar value you used in your planning becomes very important especially if you used a largely inflated amount.

Another important thing to look at in retirement is if your goal is to travel to Las Vegas once a year. In today's dollars that trip would cost approximately $3,000 a week for two people. Will you travel alone or with another couple? Do they know this and are they planning to travel in retirement as well? If they haven't included travel in their financial plan they probably will not be able to afford to go. Maybe your goal in retirement is to just play golf every day. How much is a membership? Are there any club house fees that you must incur? Maybe your goal is just to travel to your kid's homes periodically. As you can see it is important to plan for these expenditures or your travel plans could be far too expensive for you to handle.

Photcopy and fill out the following two exercises in pencil and re-evaluate every year as events in your life change and affect the end result which is usually your retirement plan. Write down your goals for retirement. Plan for them now or you will never achieve financial peace.

Exercise 15
Goals and Concerns at Retirement

Current will up to date as of _____

Living wills completed as of _____

The first two, your will and living will are mandatory and should be completed immediately. No matter your age, you're never too young if you are making an income or have some possessions you would want to leave to someone specifically.

Retirement Planning

__ Retire early and comfortably

__ Ensure my funds last through retirement

__ Leisure activities (travel, buy an RV, etc.)

__ Pay for my childs/grandchilds education

__ Reduce my income taxes

__ Preserve my estate for my beneficiaries

__ Estate Tax Planning

__ Final Expenses

__ **Other**

Listed below is an example of a typical retiree's annual expenses. This is all after tax dollars.

Example 6
Household expenses at Retirement

Property Tax $ 1500

Utilities 3600

Food 5200

Car 3600

Gas 3120

Insurance 1700
Maintenance 500
Gifts 1000
Vacation 5000
Hobbies 1000
Entertainment 2000
Medical expense 4000
TOTAL 32,220

To help you project your income in retirement, complete the following exercise. If you belong to a defined benefit pension plan, ask your employer for the calculation of how much you will earn on an annual basis when you retire. Typically the formula for a company pension income is (years of service x 2% x average of last 5 years of annual income). Your company or government will usually send you a statement periodically of how much you can expect to earn in pension income from them.

Exercise 16
Retirement Cash Flow Analysis
NET MONTHLY INCOME
Salaries   _____
Self Employed   _____
Dividend/Interest   _____
Capital Gains   _____
IRA / 401(k) / RRIF   _____
Rents/Annuities   _____
Pension/CPP/OAS   _____
Bonus/Gifts/ Misc. Inc.   _____
Alimony/Child Support   _____
Other   _____

TOTAL NET INCOME $_____

EXPENSES
DEBTS
Mortgage(s)   _____

Car Loans   _____

Credit Cards   _____

Consolidation Debts   _____

Other   _____

Total Debt Payments $_____

HOME
Rent   _____

Property Taxes   _____

Insurance   _____

Utilities   _____

Phone   _____

Cell Phone/Internet   _____

Repairs/Maintenance   _____

Total Home $_____

TRANSPORTATION
Gas   _____

Insurance   _____

Repairs/Parking   _____

Other   _____

Total Transportation $_____

INSURANCE PREMIUMS
Life   _____

Disability   _____

Health/Dental   _____

Critical Illness	_____
Other	_____
Total Insurance	$_____

DIRECT MEDICAL/DENTAL

Glasses/Prescriptions	_____
Dental	_____
Other	_____
Total Health	$_____

FLEXIBLE FAMILY NEEDS

Clothing	_____
Groceries	_____
Restaurants/Lunches	_____
Vacations/Holidays	_____
Entertainment	_____
Education/Tuition	_____
Hair/Cosmetics	_____
Child Care	_____
Subscriptions	_____
Tobacco/Alcohol	_____
Hobbies (golf, skiing, etc.)	_____
Other (gifts, charity, etc.)	_____
Total Family Needs	$_____

TOTAL INCOME $_____ - TOTAL EXPENSES $_____
AMOUNT LEFT OVER $_____

Now that you have an idea how much money you have left to live on once your expenses are paid. Let's look at how we might be able to increase that number. Below is an example of how a retiree can create extra income rather than investing in a typical Guaranteed Investment Certificate (GIC)or Bond. Tax rates for all countries are different. For this example I have picked a country with high income taxes. It is a concept that works in most countries around the world.

Example 7

An individual or couple living in Canada has a lump sum invested in a GIC or bond that they are planning to use for income through retirement. They wish to live off the income portion only and leave the principle to their children.

Let's look at some options using an amount of $300,000.

Option A
Leave the $300,000 in GIC or Bond @ 5.5% Interest
Annual Gross Income $16,500
Taxed @ 42% = $6930
Annual after tax income = $9520
Net Monthly Income = $797.50

Or

Option B
Put $300,000 into a joint and last survivor life annuity.
Annual income paid is $25,000 (partly made up from refund of principle)
Therefore only $11,000 is taxable @ 42% = $5020.63
Net Annual Income $20,503.50
Net Monthly Income $1708.63
Then purchase a $300,000 last to die permanent life

insurance policy at a cost of about $500/mn.

Now the Net Monthly Income is $1208.63 compared to $797.50 in option A

Which would you prefer?

Many people think it is taboo to speak to friends about finances, but if you are to be at peace, why not help each other. That way both families benefit and you achieve your goal. Specific dollar amounts do not necessarily have to be disclosed when discussing your financial plan with friends. It is the concepts used that lead you down the path to financial peace.

Many people assume that if I'm planning they must be too. In actual fact, only 1 in 6 people has an actual financial plan and only a few actually follow the plan that was laid out for them.

CHAPTER 14
How to Protect What You Have and Create Wealth

"To accomplish great things, we must not only act, but also dream; not only plan, but also believe."

-Henry Ford

Through out your life you will have many stages that will change your view on life and your goals. I have laid out in Figure 1. below starting at the age of 25, the path an individual's saving habits for their retirement generally follows.

25 30 35 45 50 55 60 65

Age

As you mature, you and most people, generally have common changes happen throughout their lives;

1. Buy a new car every 5 years or so.
2. Change jobs and gain or lose pension plans along the way
3. Buy a Home
4. Have Children
5. Re-negotiate mortgages
6. Maybe start a business
7. Maybe get divorced and have to start over.

All of these changes affect the amount of money we are able to put towards saving for our retirement, achieving our goals and creating wealth.

However if you are twenty five years of age and invest $315 per month at an average 8% annual rate of return and never invest less than the $315 per month you will be a millionaire by the age of 65. The older you get, the amount you need to save on a monthly or yearly basis to retire comfortably gets greater and harder to achieve. Thus, people generally get frustrated and don't try at all until it is too late.

Example 8

Let's look at what you would have to start saving to become a millionaire at 65 for different age levels.

Age	Monthly Deposit	Total Deposit	Growth	Accumulated
25	$315	$151,200	$863,440	$1,014,640
40	$1100	$330,000	$669,890	$999,890
50	$3000	$540,000	$472,819	$1,012,819

Let's say you are 45 years old. You have $60,000 in invested assets and you want to retire with a $30,000 a year income. You have no company pension plan. Old age security and other benefits may pay you $1000 a month in income. You now need to cover another $1,500 a month or $18,000 a year. To achieve that $18,000 at a conservative 6% annual rate of return, you would need to have $300,000 in invested assets when you retire.

Before you panic let's look at some ideas.

You have a small inheritance of $60,000 coming your way around the age of 50. Using the Rule of 72, determines how long it will take your money to double, let's see how that money will grow.

Rule of 72 is (72 divided by the interest you want to earn = the years needed to double.)

72 / 8 interest = 9 years

Always use a conservative interest rate of 6 to 8% annual rate of return even when in retirement.

Using an 8% rate of return; (72/8=9)

Current Investment
age 45 54 63

$60,000 doubles to $120,000 doubles to $240,000

Inheritance
age 50 59 68

$60,000 doubles to $120,000 doubles to $240,000

Using a 6% rate of return; (72/6=12)

Current Investment
age 45 57 69

$60,000 doubles to $120,000 doubles to $240,000

Inheritance
age 50 62 74

$60,000 doubles to $120,000 doubles to $240,000

As you can see the longer you wait to invest and the more conservative you are, can have a dramatic effect on your end result.

Let's look at the first option at 8% annual rate of return.

At the age of 68 your inheritance would have grown to $240,000 invested and that was with a one time deposit of $60,000. Your current invested assets of $60,000 would have grown to $240,000 by the age of 63, thus you would have approximately $480,000 at the age of 65, far exceeding the number of $300,000 that you needed to retire on. This money should be invested in a plan that meets your risk tolerance that was determined in Chapter 11.

Suppose you don't have that inheritance coming. Then again at the age of 45 you have $60,000 that will be worth approximately $240,000 at the age of 63 assuming an average annual 8% annual rate of return. You have twenty years until retirement to save that extra $60,000 dollars or approximately $3,000 a year. However it is better to save much more if you can than just meeting the $300,000 goal as future inflation, political and social events could play a dramatic part in what your retirement funds could look like.

Let's look at a leverage concept. Let's say you're 35 years of age and you borrow $20,000 every nine years and pay it off over that nine year period. How much would it add to your retirement plan? Do not worry about the interest rate at this point.

Age when money doubles	35	44	53	62
Value before borrowing	$0	$40,000	$120,000	$280,000
Borrowed amount	$20,000	$20,000	$20,000	$0
Value	$20,000	$60,000	$140,000	$280,000

As you can see there are many different ways to help you build a retirement plan. You just have to think outside the box.

A good way to protect what you have accumulated to

date is to invest in investment vehicles that protect your principle such as Guaranteed Investment Funds (GIF). You may pay a higher Management Expense Ratio (MER) of 1% to 2% but your principle will be guaranteed. These GIF funds may be 1% to 2% more expensive but you must ask yourself, "If I achieve my 6% to 8% rate of return goal and it costs me an extra 1% or 2% in fees to protect my principle is that worth it to me?" It is important to keep the end result in sight and not always worry if it costs a bit extra to get there.

Other investment vehicles such as Bonds and Guaranteed investment Certificates also known as a GIC can also help protect your principle, but at a cost. When protecting your wealth by using bonds or a GIC it is important to take advantage of a laddering technique as inflation and taxes will take a big portion of your gains. It is also important to note that not all bonds are 100% guaranteed. Know what you are purchasing.

Example 10

Let's say you have $20,000 to invest, the laddering technique works as follows;

Purchase 5 separate GIC's at $4,000 each and ladder the maturity dates. Interest rates are only for the purpose of the example.

1 year $4,000 at 2.8%
2 year $4,000 at 3.1%
3 year $4,000 at 3.4%
4 year $4,000 at 3.75%
5 year $4,000 at 4.1%
or

Purchase 4 separate bonds and ladder the maturity dates as follows; again the interest rate is for example purposes only.

5 year $5,000 bond at 4%

10 year $5,000 bond at 6%

15 year $5000 bond at 8%

20 year $5,000 bond at 10%

By using this technique your principle is protected and you always have an investment coming due to take advantage of interest rate changes. An important fact to remember about bonds is that they are not always 100% guaranteed. Know what you are buying. Also, when interest rates are low, bonds are very expensive to purchase, and even though you might be able to purchase a 10 year bond at 6% what is the actual yield of the bond when it matures?

Example 11

Your 10 year 6% Bond cost you $102 per unit to buy. However when it matures you will on receive $100 per unit. Therefore your yield is less than the 6% rate you expect.

To buy $10,000 Bond at $102 = 98.04 units.

At maturity you receive $100 x 98.04 units = $9,804

Therefore, when purchasing a bond, ask what the yield is. If you are 75 years of age and you purchase a 20 year bond at 8%, I don't really think you need to care about the yield unless you are concerned about your surviving spouse or children needing this money to live off for their retirement also.

CHAPTER 15
Conclusion

Using these techniques leading up to and in retirement will help you protect your wealth while still helping you slowly, create wealth.

Having completed all the exercises in this book I hope you have realized what it is you truly want out of life and that you have a plan on how to get there.

Open the envelope from the first exercise. Read aloud the obituary you wrote. Do the goals or path you set for yourself, lead someone to write a similar obituary when you pass away.

On the next page is your plan, transcribe your numbers and required information to help you visualize what your life is like, where you are, and what you need to improve. Put this in a place that is visual to you on a daily basis such as a mirror in you bedroom or you closet door.

YOUR PLAN
What is prosperity to you?

_____

What is financial peace to you?

_____

Prosperity Goals Financial Goals Retirement Goals

_____   _____   _____

_____   _____   _____

Risk Tolerance_____
Expected retirement Age____

Balance sheet Cash Flow $
Assets_____ Income_____
Liabilities_____ Expenses_____
Net Worth_____ Uncommitted Income_____
Emergency Fund_____
Investments Balance_____
Life Insurance_____   _____

_____ _____

Child's Education account Balance_____
Goals account Balance_____
Retirement Dollars Needed _____

YESTERDAY – TODAY – TOMORROW

"Yesterday is but a dream, tomorrow is only a vision. But today, well lived makes every tomorrow a vision of hope. Look well, therefore, to this day, for it is life, the very life of life."

-The Sanskrit

I thank you for taking the time to read this book and please share the knowledge you have gained with as many people as you can about how to create prosperity and financial peace.

-Graham Howarth

www.ingramcontent.com/pod-product-compliance
Lightning Source LLC
Chambersburg PA
CBHW022113210326
41597CB00047B/516